A Short Guide to
Authenticity

by
Joshua J. Tilley

Introduction

What do you do after you write a doctoral thesis? You write a book. Who do you write it for? For the tens of people who do deep study and aggressive research...and here you are. Welcome.

My goal here was to write a short concise academic book detailing one aspect of my thesis: authenticity. My original essay and research was completed by conducting a phenomenology on authentic leadership, but through the study I found the current academic research lacking a basic model of authenticity proper, so I was forced to create one. As long as the research is already done, I have decided to share it with you.

I created my model based upon existential philosophy, logos therapy, my background in philosophy, theology, ancient Greek, and the current research surrounding the topic of authenticity itself. If you find the information helpful, you can always read the original research in its entirety. The thesis can be found here...

https://rim.atla.com/index.php/node/37110

I hope that this model finds an application in your studies.

Good luck!

Joshua Tilley

Chapter 1
Why Authenticity Matters

Shakespeare wrote tragedies, comedies, and tales of wisdom but what many do not realize is that he was also a top notch philosopher.[1] In one of his most well-known dramas, Hamlet, we are introduced to a young man by the name of Laertes. He is leaving home and his father, Polonius, takes this opportunity to pass on a tiny morsel of his wisdom onto his son. It is in this moment where we receive the eternal words, "This above all: to thine own self be true."[2]

It is based upon these words that many scholars define authenticity. Using Laertes as motivation, one author explained that authentic people "are true to themselves, are consistent in their beliefs, words, and actions."[3] This definition definitely has the ring of authenticity, but this was not what Shakespeare meant.

Today with all the hustle and bustle, it seems like wise counsel indeed to take a moment to, above all else, be true to one's self. We all desperately struggle and strive in our information addicted society hoping for something real to grasp.[4] We all want something absolute and authentic to live by and to believe in. This truth, to be true to yourself, is often sold as the core of authenticity and, it is believed, this maxim is our only hope of living a life of peace. The reality is that living authentically is deeper, more

---

[1] William Hazlitt, www. Absoluteshakespeare.com, https://absoluteshakespeare.com/guides/essays/othello_characters_essay.htm (accessed Oct 1, 2018).

[2] Shakespeare, Hamlet, Act 1, Scene 3, lines 560-565.

[3] Anna Elisabeth Weischer, Jürgen Weibler, and Malte Petersen, "'To Thine own Self be True': The Effects of Enactment and Life Storytelling on Perceived Leader Authenticity," *Leadership Quarterly* 24 (2013): 477.

[4] Edwin H. Friedman, Margaret M. Treadwell, and Edward W. Beal. *A Failure of Nerve: Leadership in the Age of the Quick Fix*. New York: Church Publishing, 2017, 110.

complex, and much more robust than simply being true to yourself. This is a common misconception surrounding authenticity.

The above quote comes from a leadership journal article claiming, "The roots of the concept of authenticity lie in an aphorism derived from Greek philosophy and expounded by Shakespeare's Polonius: 'To thine own self be true.'"[5] Sadly this is only one example of this distorted story. We know this, because this was not Shakespeare's point at all. Some scholars and laypeople seem to entirely miss the context of Hamlet and this statement.

With a cursory exegetical study, one comes to find that Polonius is not the wise old man we are led to believe. Such a judgment is simply the reader's decision to ignore the context in order to get what they want from the text. This is an exegetical mistake called the "pleasure principle."[6] The truth is that Laertes is far from authentic.

Those who want to see these snippets of advice as wisdom are inclined to conclude this man has a depth of a knowledge beyond our grasp and a wisdom for the ages, but in its context what Shakespeare actually wants us to understand is that Polonius is a bumbling idiot. In the story, Laertes tries to avoid his father. He heard his father's voice and immediately tries to find sanctuary in order to avoid the old man's incessant babbling. At no point in Shakespeare's *Hamlet* is Polonius portrayed as or considered wise. By extension, these words were never meant to be a mantra for living, these are examples of shallow human wisdom.

This is the telltale work of Shakespeare's irony at its best as he puts perceivably the most "wise" words into the mouth of the most simple character. Farahmandfar and Samigorganroodi write, "Shakespeare depicts authenticity in the character of Hamlet, and it is in contrast to him that the reader finds many instances of

---

[5] Anna Elisabeth Weischer, "'To Thine Own Self be True,'" 477.

[6] Kevin Vanhoozer, *Is There a Meaning in This Text?: the Bible, the Reader, and the Morality of Literary Knowledge.* Grand Rapids, MI: Zondervan, 1998, 38.

*in*authenticity."[7] To assume this is advice to be followed is to miss the point: Polonius himself is an example of *in*authenticity and his words are the definition of this *in*authentic life. This aphorism actually comes at the end of a long list of cliches meant to sound wise, but with all the depth of a teaspoon. This can be easily tested and proven.

The fact is that if applied and taken at face value, the diatribe concerning "self above all else" would create the most evil of egotist or the greatest of megalomaniacs. Based upon the evidence, the reader can discern that Polonius is the antithesis of our hero, Hamlet, whose "main challenge is to live authentically."[8] With a bit of reasoning, we can see that the idea of being true to yourself above all else would be to cast aside family and friends for one's own selfish ambition and happiness. This falls short of authenticity as something must balance personal truth and selfishness cannot be authentic. Consider an authentic leader.

The authentic leader should not be selfish. Also, an authentic leader does more than simply lead. According to current research, authenticity is the difference between someone who is simply in charge and someone who is actually perceived as "good" by their subordinates.[9] Authentic people are followed intentionally not just because they are in charge. This feeling is even transferred to their followers.[10] So what essence of authenticity?

---

[7] Masoud Farahmandfar and Gholamreza Samigorganroodi, "'To Thine Own Self Be True': Existentialism in *Hamlet* and *The Blind Owl*," *International Journal of Comparative Literature & Translation Studies*, Vol. 3 No. 2; (April 2015): 25.

[8] Farahmandfar, "To Thine Own Self Be True," 25.

[9] Sandu Frunză, "Seeking Meaning, Living Authenticity and Leadership in Public Space. A Philosophical Perspective," *Transylvanian Review of Administrative Sciences*, no. 52E (2017): 31.

[10] Melissa S. Cardon, "Is Passion Contagious? The Transference of Entrepreneurial Passion to Employees." *Human Resource Management Review* 18, no. 2 (2008): 77–86: 79.

Chapter 2
The Origin of Authenticity

I came to develop this model through the use of what is known as a phenomenological study (For more information see Appendix 1). A phenomenological study was chosen because it is interested in the "diversity of human experience"[11] based both in the past and present. Phenomenologies require one to start broad and to slowly narrow their focus,[12] therefore my research began broadly with the oldest known use of the word "authentic."

The Greek word αὐθεντικὸς has its original sense in "self" (autos) and "being" (hentes) and is often translated as "authoritative."[13] This use can be seen in the Gnostic text, αὐθεντικὸς λόγος (Authoritative Teaching).[14] Despite the text never being widely accepted by the Church,[15] it is a testimony to the words earliest known use. In this text αὐθεντικὸς can either be understood as a "speech of authority," a text which is an "authentic presentation" of a tradition, or it can be used in the sense of being an "original copy" of an authoritative document.[16]

This is a positive use of the word as the origin in question is assumed to be good and wise. By extension, the teaching presented in the text itself is just as good and wise as the authority

---

[11] Max Van Manen, "Phenomenology in Its Original Sense," *Qualitative Health Research* , Vol. 27(6), (2017): 810 –825: 146.

[12] Van Manen, "Phenomenology in Its Original Sense," 75.

[13] _____, "Authentic (Adj.)." Etymology Online, http://www.etymonline.com/word/authentic (accessed June 12, 2018).

[14] George W. MacRae (translator), *Authoritative Teaching -- The Nag Hammadi Library*. www.gnosis.org. http://gnosis.org/naghamm/autho.html (accessed July 1 2018).

[15] C.T. Friedeman, "Authoritative Teaching," *The Lexham Bible Dictionary* (Bellingham, WA: Lexham Press, 2016).

[16] 3. subst., αὐ. τό, original copy, PFam.Teb.31.13 (ii A.D.), v. ἔκβασος.

from which it was either given or inspired by. A modern comparison would be a piece of legislation signed into law by the president. The expectation is that the authority of the president would be transferred to the text itself as if the transcript itself were equal to the authority it represents.

Elsewhere αὐθεντικὸς is often found to be used in a negative sense. When the word was used by one individual against another, it was always used negatively, being translated as being "heavy handed" or "prideful."[17] In Euripides' play, *The Trojan Women*, the word is used in reference to her husband's "murderer."[18] This word was also used by Basil where the action was in reference to the "anathematization of Dianius."[19] In yet another instance the word was used by Chrysostom as a warning to husbands to not "abuse" their wives.[20] The examples continue as the negative uses of αὐθέντῃ often imply treachery, "murder," and/or "violence."[21]

Because of this, Cynthia Westfall argues this word was only ever positively applied to individuals who were understood to have some form of ultimate or unquestionable authority such as an god or the Catholic pope. Westfall argues that this change of usage may have been deliberate. She believes this was done by the Catholic Church to establish papal authority through a comparison

---

[17] Cynthia Long Westfall, "The Meaning of αὐθεντέω in 1 Timothy 2:12," *Journal of Greco-Roman Christianity and Judaism*, 10 (2014), 147.

[18] Euripides, "The Trojan Women by Euripides," *The Internet Classics Archive*. www. classics.mit.edu. http://classics.mit.edu/Euripides/troj_women.html, (accessed June 24, 2018).

[19] Westfall, "The Meaning of αὐθεντέω in 1 Timothy 2:12," 166.

[20] John Chrysostom, Hom. Matt. 57:239. 45-54.

[21] _____, "αὐθέντῃ." *Greek Word Study Tool*. Perseus Digital Library. www.perseus.tufts.edu.

http://www.perseus.tufts.edu/hopper/morph?l=au%29qe%2Fnths&la=greek&can=au%29qe%2Fnths0#lexicon (accessed June 15, 2018).

of the pope with God.[22] According to Westfall's research, αὐθεντικὸς was only ever considered to be good when applied to those with obvious authority over others. The problem with this hypothesis is it ignores the earlier uses in reference to Caesar and even the extension of such authority as seen at Qumran.

Westfall seems to either ignore or be ignorant of the evidence that this word does in fact find positive usage as can be seen in the writings of Cicero when he used it in reference to news he received on "good authority." In one instance, Cicero explained he believes and trusts that Caesar will bring much needed judgment upon Carbo and Brutus. It is because of his trust that he deems the information to be "good."

This trust is later confirmed when both men were brought to justice and killed as promised.[23] In addition, the word is used when Pompey is set to invade "Germany by way of Illyricum"; again this news was trusted on "good authority."[24] As can be seen through mankind's earliest use of the word, authority and αὐθεντικὸς have always gone hand in hand and such authority could we shared by man and god alike.

---

[22] Westfall, "The Meaning of αὐθεντέω in 1 Timothy 2:12," 159.

[23] Cicero and E. Shuckburgh (Ed.), *The Letters of Cicero: the Whole Extant Correspondence in Chronological Order in Four Volumes* (Medford, MA: George Bell and Sons, 1909), 347.

[24] Cicero, *The Letters of Cicero*, 384.

Chapter 3
The Benefits of Authenticity

Scientific studies have shown a direct correlation between perceived authenticity and several benefits. For example, leaders who are believed to be "authentic" are understood by their followers to be more "responsible,"[25] "ethical,"[26] and "in control of their moods."[27] Authenticity is often seen as the number one difference between a good effective leader and a basic overseer. Sandu Frunza explained, "We tend to attribute the quality of leadership to those managers who prove to be bearers of the marks of authenticity."[28] The benefits do not end with the perceiver.

Leaders who are identified as authentic score higher in tests of "emotional intelligence, self-monitoring ability, and political skill."[29] With this emotional intelligence comes the display of authentic emotions, which have been linked to a contagious sense of passion.[30] This has a strong effect on the "creativity, persistence, and absorption" of the follower, which leads to people setting more challenging goals, using more creativity in tackling those challenges, and persisting longer in tasks, even when overcoming obstacles.

---

[25] R. Edward Freeman and Ellen R. Auster. "Values, Authenticity, and Responsible Leadership." *Responsible Leadership* (2011): 15–23: 16.

[26] Frunză, "Seeking Meaning, Living Authenticity and Leadership in Public Space," 29.

[27] William L. Gardner, Dawn Fischer, and James G. Hunt, "Emotional Labor and Leadership: A Threat to Authenticity?," *The Leadership Quarterly* 20 (2009): 467.

[28] Frunza, 31.

[29] Gardner, "Emotional Labor and Leadership," 476-477.

[30] Melissa S. Cardon, "Is Passion Contagious? The Transference of Entrepreneurial Passion to Employees," 79.

This gives entrepreneurs the power to do whatever it takes to realize their visions, to guide their thoughts, actions, and to work on tasks with tenacity. This includes an improved success rate when followers "pitch their ideas" and when they solicit investors to "raise funds from venture capitalists."[31] Based upon the evidence, authenticity creates an environment for winners.

Such leaders also have a better grasp of who they are as individuals. Freeman and Auster explain, "living authentically means asking hard questions about [one's own] aspirations, not taking them at face value, understanding the connections to past, present, and future that they are based on."[32] This pursuit leads to an increase in the leader's own "felt authenticity" as well as "the favorability of follower impressions, and the perceived authenticity of the leader by the followers."

The benefits continue as the "authenticity of the leader impacts the favorability of followers' impressions and subsequent trust in the leader. Furthermore, leaders experience feelings of relative authenticity, which, in turn, relate to their overall sense of well-being."[33] Current research further suggests authenticity is beneficial for not just those who perceive it, but also for the individual who lives it.[34] As testified by Cicero and supported by modern scholarship,[35] trust must accompany a leader if their authority is to be considered authentic.

When confronted with this new research many scholars are reconsidering authenticity. These scholars are rejecting the concept

---

[31] Cardon, "Is Passion Contagious?" 78.

[32] Freeman, "Values, Authenticity, and Responsible Leadership," 21.

[33] Gardner, "Emotional Labor and Leadership," 468.

[34] Deana M. Raffo, "Reflection and Authentic Leadership (Chapter Eight)." In *Leading with Spirit, Presence, and Authenticity: A Volume in the International Leadership Association Series Building Leadership Bridges*, Edited by Kathryn Goldman Schuyler. John Wiley & Sons, Incorporated, 2014. ProQuest Ebook Central. 182.

[35] Gardner, 468.

of authenticity as a quality and embracing authenticity as a process one chooses.[36] Freeman and Auster explain, "We see authenticity as a creative project, one where we strive to create a life imbued with the process of trying to live in an authentic way."[37]

They continue, "Being conscious of that freedom when choosing to realize a particular project is the real meaning of authenticity." As a result some researchers have come to redefine the authentic leaders as those who know who they are and what they believe in; display transparency and consistency among their values, ethical reasoning, and actions; focus on developing positive psychological states such as confidence, optimism, hope, and resilience within themselves and their associates; and are widely known and respected for their integrity.[38]

This evidence shows us that authenticity is a form of existence. It is an aspect of being which must be pursued. It is a process and contrary to the belief that the key is "being true to yourself," it requires trust to be accepted and embraced.

As we rightfully reject the shallow definition of authenticity that we read on social media and in the form of countless tattoos, four aspects of authenticity rise from the ashes...

---

[36] Freeman, 19.

[37] Freeman, 16.

[38] Susan Skjei, "Leaders' Lived Experience of Authentic Moments (Chapter Ten)," *Leading with Spirit, Presence, and Authenticity: A Volume in the International Leadership Association Series Building Leadership Bridges,* Kathryn Goldman Schuyler (ed) (John Wiley & Sons, Incorporated, 2014. ProQuest Ebook Central), 213.

Chapter 4
The Four Aspects of Authenticity

The Situation

Authenticity is not perceived in a vacuum. Authenticity transcends cultures, belongs to groups and individuals,[39] and is ontological,[40] but despite its paradoxical connection to and transcendence of this world it can still be grasped as a single moment. This getting to the "heart of things" is called the "kairos moment" by phenomenologist Max Van Manen.[41] Every moment that provokes this intuition or feeling of authenticity involves the Situation one finds themself in.

These events happen in a place and are perceived through a subcultural lens, which is eventually interpreted in contrast to the follower's own history and past experiences all of which encompass an individual's worldview and life. This same understanding plays out in both the modern and ancient uses because authenticity pertains to the context as well as the players in our world and our situation. These experiences and situations create trust as they are confirmed to be trustworthy over time.

For this reason, Cicero "trusts" the news of Pompey's invasion of Germany based upon authority. We see this same trust played out in other scientific studies as "the favorability of follower impressions of a leader are positively related to follower's trust in the leader."[42] As the study continues it becomes apparent that the context and Situation are more and more prominent in the perception and application of authenticity and that this trust is situationally dependent.

---

[39] Andrew J. Pierce, "Authentic Identities." *Social Theory and Practice* 41, no. 3 (2015): 442-443: 436.

[40] Farahmandfar, "To Thine Own Self Be True," 26.

[41] Van Manen, "Phenomenology in Its Original Sense," 822.

[42] Gardner, "Emotional Labor and Leadership," 472

As we dig deeper, the existential nature of authenticity becomes apparent. In the case of leadership, researchers argue that the perception of authenticity in the follower and the feeling of being authentic in the leader themself are both partially dependent upon the Situation as "context is domain specific" (see figure 1). Therefore, all studies of authenticity must take into consideration the Situation as a person must be able "to accurately gauge the emotional norms of the situation" in order to act authentically.[43]

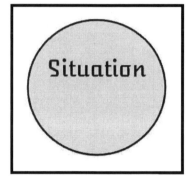

Figure 1. The situation.

Authenticity must embrace and act within the confines of the world in which leaders and followers live, otherwise the action could be misconstrued as "phony," "inauthentic," "hypocritical," "disingenuous," and or lacking sincerity.[44] The Situation provides the background, foreground, and stage for all events and this aspect of the existential nature of authenticity.

The Other

As an endeavour, authenticity requires an understanding of the perceptions and judgments of others. For leaders, ideas such as being considered "arrogant," "humble," or "confident" only have value in the face of others without which there would be nothing to be arrogant, humble, or confident about. For this reason, the Self and the Other provide the content and the world or Situation provides the context.[45] Almost all concepts lack meaning outside of

---

[43] Gardner, "Emotional Labor and Leadership," 472.

[44] Gardner, 467.

[45] Charles Taylor, *The Ethics of Authenticity*. Cambridge: Belknap Press, 1991, 49.

an Other to reflect the action back upon (see Figure 2), a rejection of this can result in social atomism.[46]

A rejection of the Other can drive one to become "more entrenched" in an instrumental stance resulting in anthropocentrism, which creates a moral nihilism where the Other becomes an object and a means to an end.[47] Any such denial of the Other results in a "fragmentation" of identity, which can cause the destruction of sympathy and the creation of selfishness.[48] Therefore, if selfishness is the motivation, the action will be perceived as negative or "phony" and it is deemed to be *inauthentic*.

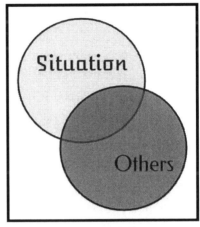

Figure 2. The situation and others.

As a result of this raw potentiality, with the Other also comes doubt,[49] anxiety,[50] and shame.[51] But despite the many difficulties that arise, the Other is an inevitability which must be considered. As the Other is here to

---

[46] https://plato.stanford.edu/entries/social-ontology/#Atom

[47] Taylor, 59-6.

[48] Taylor, 113.

[49] Benjamin Young, "A Qualitative Study of Doubt in the Evangelical Tradition," DMin Thesis, Bethel Seminary, St. Paul, 2015. Accessed March 21, 2018. CLIC Thesis (9910123312903692).

Leo Tolstoy and Jane Kentish, *A Confession and Other Religious Writings* (Harmondsworth, Middlesex, England: Penguin, 1987), 118.

[50] David E. Roberts, *Psychotherapy and a Christian View of Man* (New York: Charles Scribner's Sons, 1950), 46-47.

[51] Lewis B. Smedes, *Shame and Grace: Healing the Shame We Don't Deserve* (Harper San Francisco, 1993), 17-27.

stay, "life can seem easier if you reject morality," but to do so is to not live authentically.[52] Though the Other will at times be *embraced* and at other times *tolerated*, each individual must accept their commitment to the Other if they are to be authentic.

With the Other ethics comes into view[53] opening up the mind of the individual to a realm of metaphysical commitments they did not consider before the encounter. Through modern research, in conjunction with the ancient understandings of authenticity considered earlier, it seems this ethical consideration and commitment to others should be the driving force which guides the lives, words, and actions of authentic people. Being authentic must include taking this call to the Other seriously.

The Other and the Self are both equally involved in the authentic moment and its interpretation, therefore ethics must also be considered when determining an action to be authentic.[54] For this reason, a negative evaluation or condemnation of the Other will only be usurped if the need for ethical justice is higher. Based upon this, extremes such as allowing one's Self to be harmed or harming another can actually be deemed authentic (seen as self-sacrifice or self-defense) despite the harm to the Other or the self. In this way, authenticity is deeper than mere actions and therefore an emergent and transcendent property, which coexists with ethics.

As a transcendent property, authenticity is not an ideal hidden within the essence of a thing, but rather an ideal found above and beyond the object. The object itself is a raw potentiality seated within the ontological commitments contained within to the Self, the Other, and the Situation they find themselves in. In the case of human authenticity, the Self and Other can make a

---

[52] Taylor, *The Ethics of Authenticity*, 57.

[53] Aristotle, *The Nicomachean Ethics*, 50.

[54] Frunza, "Seeking Meaning, Living Authenticity and Leadership," 29.

comparison to this ideal and judge its credibility based upon the "original way of being human."[55]

The decision to pursue authenticity therefore finds its basis in ethical responsibility as one's freedom is one's transcendence; (i.e. "the ghost in the machine").[56] Inevitably, authenticity is not a state of being, but rather an all encompassing human endeavour. As all truth follows from the existence of the thing itself,[57] authenticity becomes the ontological pursuit of the human essence and the ideal which it "images." According to this understanding, authenticity is found in those fleeting moments when the Situation, the Other, and the Self align for the same purpose and with the same meaning.

The Self

The Self must live despite one's limits. Authenticity demands individuals make free choices independent of outside pressures and anxiety, but such a course of action could be grounded in deception if one is insincere.[58] Every individual must sincerely consider their responsibilities to the Other, which are part of our natural limits. This ethical commitment permeates every authentic decision because others can never be used as an end in themselves; such an action negates the authentic human aspect of a choice, being that all human beings are equally human ontologically. To deny human equality, at least in the sense of being equally human, would be to live inauthentically, because to do so would be to live a lie. Therefore the action must consider the Other before being executed.

---

[55] Taylor, *The Ethics of Authenticity*, 61.

[56] Michael S. Gazzianiga and Megan Steven, *Neuroscience and the Law: Brain, Mind, and the Scales of Justice* (New York, NY: Dana Press, 2005), 52-54.

[57] Jacques Maritain and Galantiere Lewis, *Existence and the Existent* (Garden City, NY: Image Books, 1956), 20-21.

[58] Gardner, "Emotional Labor and Leadership," 471.

In this understanding, authenticity must center itself between the poles of selfishness (treating others as objects) and martyrdom (treating one's Self as an "object-for-others" as Sartre explains). Authentic action seeks an equilibrium and strives to balance the ethical commitments which naturally occur. This is an ontological problem found in all human agency. It is the struggle between love, justice, and power.[59]

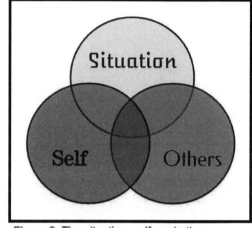

Figure 3. The situation, self, and others.

When done authentically, such a struggle has been shown to create trust for both the Self and the Other. This balancing act within relationships is referred to as the "rhythm of rightness"[60] because the power struggle between the Self and Other is in a constant state of flux and realignment. When pursued, this leads to self-efficacy[61] and humility (see figure 3).

As authenticity is a process without the luxury of measurable progress, this level of uncertainty needs to be approached with courage[62] wherein one embraces the necessary

[59] Paul Tillich, *Love, Power, Justice*. Cambridge: Oxford Press, 1960: 2.

[60] Terry D. Hargrave and Franz Pfitzer, *Restoration Therapy: Understanding and Guiding Healing in Marriage and Family Therapy* (Brunner-Routledge, 2011), 37.

[61] Albert *Bandura*. "Self-Efficacy Defined." www.uky.edu. http://www.uky.edu/~eushe2/Bandura/BanEncy.html (accessed July 1, 2018).

[62] Paul Tillich, *The Courage to Be* (New Haven, CT: Yale University Press, 1952), 23.

limits. This keeps "the human mind from voyaging into the delusion of omniscience"[63] which reinforces the humility needed to grow. One must make an effort to differentiate between one's ideals and goals from that of the Other.[64] The inability to know the difference can cause shame and hinder growth.[65] The ideal is authenticity and the goal must be maturity and growth itself.

Next the problem is to determine what the purpose of this growth is. The only answer can be true authentic humanness. Only in defining the goal as growth into "essential humanness" can one avoid the shame of mistakes while still embracing the confession and repentance necessary for progress as all such action "presupposes participation in something which transcends the self."[66] Maturity requires a willingness to admit mistakes and grow from them.

Paradoxically, the acceptance of forgiveness for one's Self and granting forgiveness to the Other becomes a part of the journey as both the shame of guilt and the anger of revenge hinder progress.[67] Choosing one's course forces a change of perception and this transcendence and forgiveness is the only option.[68] The daily struggle of choosing authenticity can reframe even our failures into an adventure providing excitement[69] which forces the

---

[63] Friedman, "*A Failure of Nerve*," 52.

[64] Gardner, "Emotional Labor and Leadership," 467.

[65] Smedes, *Shame and Grace, 9-10.*

[66] Tillich, *The Courage to Be*, 165.

[67] Smedes, 135.

[68] Marjorie Grene, "Authenticity: An Existential Virtue," *Ethics*, Vol. LXII, July 1952, 266.

[69] Maritain, *Existence and the Existent*, 74.

Friedman, *A Failure of Nerve*, 200.

myth of Sisyphus[70] to be redefined as a journey of "self-discovery and artistic creation."[71] This is embodied in the pursuit of full humanhood.

This is ontological and it must be understood that to know an essence is to search for "that which a thing is,"[72] but as authenticity is here defined as the pursuit of essential humanness, it does not come naturally. The problem is that one's own essence is perceived as a subject through one's own consciousness, imposing a separation of objectivity dependent upon one's own subjectivity,[73] but this is not a lost cause.

In authenticity, humanity sees the kairos it is in as a struggle, but this perceived hell (Sartre) can be recaptured as an adventure (Tillich) if one embraces the pursuit of what it means to be fully human. In this way, one's own responsibility is the journey. In reference to the ethical standards found in leadership, Robert Greenleaf explained, "This self-respect and integrity, in turn, produces the ability to be both kind and courageous with other people-kind in showing a great respect and reverence for other people, their view, feelings, experiences, and convictions, but also courageous in expressing their own convictions without personal threat."[74] This courage is essential to the process of

---

[70] In the myth of Sisyphus, Albert Camus saw a metaphor for human existence. He believed that life was a constant struggle with no end in sight. In this sense every human being is doomed to create meaning, but when authenticity is pursued the feeling of doom can be redeemed into a journey of discovery.

The myth is explained in Camus, *The Myth of Sisyphus,* 64.

[71] Taylor, *The Ethics of Authenticity*, 61.

[72] Maritain, 70.

[73] Maritain, *Existence and the Existent,* 76-77.

[74] Robert K. Greenleaf and Larry C. Spears, *"Servant Leadership: a Journey into the Nature of Legitimate Power and Greatness"* (Paulist Press, 2002), loc 70-175.

becoming authentic.[75] This perception of the world, be it hell or adventure, is dependent upon one's metaphysical commitments and worldview.

Which brings the reader full circle to one of the original uses of αὐθεντικὸς; used in the positive sense αὐθεντικὸς imparts the authenticity of the original copy of an authoritative document onto its copy.[76] Just as Cicero's news was only as valuable as the authority behind it, authenticity is only authentic by comparison to its ideal. Similarly, for Plato, all objects in the world were seen to be only as "good" as they reflected the perfection of the forms.[77]

Therefore, a person is only authentic by comparison to what it means to be essentially human. As such, the essence of mankind is the goal and authenticity is measured by this ideal alone. All pursuit of this perfection begins with this image. This pursuit is subjectively chosen (as a worldview), but can, by the above criteria, be objectively judged. For this reason, the authentic person must act in such a way as to accurately and effectively meet the ethical requirements which pertain to the Other, are relevant to the Self, and which fit within the confines of the Situation; all of which are guided and maintained within one's metaphysic and metanarrative.

---

[75] Tillich, *The Courage to Be*, 139.

[76] H.G. Liddell and R. Scott, *A Greek-English Lexicon* (Oxford: Clarendon Press, 1996), 275.

[77] One does not need to ascribe to Platonism to understand the analogy.

Chapter 5
Authenticity: Becoming More Human

Through the review it became abundantly clear that no one is ever perfectly authentic all the time and in all situations. As authenticity is dependent upon multiple factors, I came to understand that authenticity is a process. This is why, when confronted with the most recent research, many scholars are reconsidering authenticity. Most current studies are now rejecting the idea of authenticity simply as a quality and embracing it as a process one chooses.[78]

As Robert Freeman and Ellen Auster explained, "We see authenticity as a creative project, one where we strive to create a life imbued with the process of trying to live in an authentic way." [79] They continue, "Being conscious of that freedom when choosing to realize a particular project is the real meaning of authenticity." Rollo May would most likely concur as he believed, "The existential approach puts decision and will back into the center of the picture."[80] The pursuit of authenticity requires the transcendence of humanity as one chooses to live despite the Situation.

This ability to look down upon one's own experience and choose a course was considered essential to the earliest philosophical writers. Heraclitus, a pre-socratic philosopher, explained "thinking is common to all," therefore philosophers must choose to search out the truth, because "nature loves to hide."[81] Seneca explained, "We are all chained to Fortune. Some chains are golden and loose, some tight and of base metal; but what

---

[78] Freeman, "Values, Authenticity, and Responsible Leadership," 19.

[79] Freeman, 16.

[80] May, *Existential Psychology*, 43.

[81] Marc S. Cohen, Patricia Curd, C.D.C. Reeve (Eds), *Reading in Ancient Greek Philosophy*. 2nd ed, (Indianapolis, IN: Hackett Publishing Company, Inc., 2000), 27-28.

difference does it make?" He goes on to explain that despite fate, humans must still choose what they can. He continued, "All life is bondage. Man must therefore habituate himself to his condition, complain of it as little as possible, and grasp whatever good lies within his reach."[82]

The ability to take into consideration one's Self, one's relationship to the Other, and the Situation itself are the stuff of philosophers as these concepts were discussed by Socrates, argued by Plato, and debated by the later empiricists and rationalists. C.S. Lewis explained, "What we learn from experience depends on the kind of philosophy we bring to the experience."[83] David W. Clark explained, "Philosophy clarifies the modes of reflection, and, as such, it is useful to theology."[84] This brings the reader to the realization that one's metaphysical commitments can and do shape one's perception of the world, therefore such commitments must be chosen as they will inherently shape one's perception and influence one's decisions. Choice and the responsibility for that choice are therefore necessary in the pursuit of authenticity.

Not all agree. Bertrand Russell held that the concept of free will is a religious idea often used to instill fear rather than freedom,[85] but this does not change the importance of one's ability to transcend their experience and choose. Avid and outspoken atheist, John Dewey, strongly disagreed with such an opinion. He wrote, "It is, then, a sound instinct which identifies freedom with power to frame purposes and to execute or carry into effect purposes so framed."

---

[82] Seneca, *The Stoic Philosophy of Seneca: Essays and Letters of Seneca*, (London: The Norton Library, 1968), 93.

[83] C.S. Lewis, *Miracles: A Preliminary Study*, (New York: Harper Collins, 2001), 2.

[84] Clark, "A Preliminary Investigation and Critique of the Ethics of Dietrich Bonhoeffer," 40.

[85] Bertrand Russell, *Why I am Not a Christian: and other essays on religion and related subjects*, (New York: George Allen & Unwin LTD, 1957), 39-41.

23

He explained that anyone who does not embrace their freedom are slaves.[86] Noted philosopher, Steven Pinker, concurs explaining that we all frame our experience through our worldview and this framing shapes our experience.[87] The question is, can someone get to the core and essential nature of an experience, despite one's worldview influencing them? Phenomenology says, yes. Transcendence of one's worldview, though difficult, is possible.

This ability to transcend and consider outside influences is what separates humankind from the animals. Aristotle called human beings "rational animals" saying that the key to the virtues was the practice of justice, courage, and the like. It is only in choosing to practice that one becomes virtuous.[88]

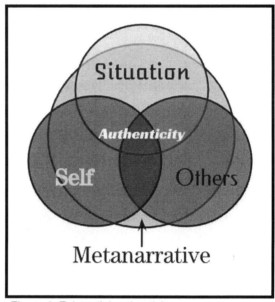

Figure 4. Existential authenticity.

Through this knowledge we can see the importance of creating a model for understanding all aspects of authenticity. Such information can only be viewed through action if one is to attempt

---

[86] John Dewey, *Experience and Education*, (New York: Simon & Schuster, 1997), 67.

[87] Steven Pinker, *The Stuff of Thought: Language as a Window into Human Nature*, (New York: Viking, 2007), 260-261.

[88] Aristotle, James Alexander, Kerr Thomson, Hugh Tredennick, and Jonathan Barnes. *The Nicomachean Ethics*. London: Penguin Books, 2004., 31-38.

to be a part of the process of becoming authentic. This led to the creation of a model of authenticity proper (figure 4). Here the Situation, Other, and Self are seen to intersect with authenticity being the intersection of each aspect of the individual, but here we see the addition of the individual's metaphysic/worldview. As this model reveals, it is only in the intersection of these three aspects, guided by one's metaphysic, where the potential for authenticity emerges.

Max van Manen explains the importance of models. He wrote,

> Models are like phenomenological examples. So, to reflect in a hermeneutic phenomenological manner on the meaning of some object is to examine it as an originary model. Some models are more appropriate or better suited to get at the originary meaning of objects. And so, models must be well chosen as interpretive examples because the essence of the object has to be in the model.[89]

Rollo May gives a real life example of how the Situation, Other, and Self come together for the benefit of the patient. Arguing for this existential connection between the authentic therapist and patient he wrote,

> This can be seen clearly in the relationship between a client and a therapist. The goal of the therapist is to enter the Situation the client finds their Self in and enter this story as an authentic self. The Other remains other, but an I and Thou relationship ensues as the Other is understood to be their own real Self in this shared situation. It is only in this way that the client can 'discover what is real in him.'[90]

Here one can grasp a real life scenario wherein one might use the

---

[89] Van Manen, *Phenomenology of Practice,* 186.

[90] Rollo May, *Existential Psychology.* New York: Random House, 1969. 88.

above existential model and help others to see authenticity is an emergent property which rises up from the collision and conflict found in one's everyday experience and existence.

Chapter 6
The Effects of Authenticity

Here I outline some of the details of my research on authentic leadership that was published elsewhere. As this book is meant to be an introduction to authenticity proper, I will only provide a few points to highlight the effect of authenticity in a real world application. My hope is to spur on more people to apply this model to new avenues of study in order to further their research.

I tested my theory of authenticity on a "heterogeneous group" of individuals. A phenomenology was conducted to discover the experience of "authentic leadership" in action. Through field notes, recorded conversations, and transcribed interviews I was able to identify significant statements. These lengthy interviews were broken down into notes and these notes were further distilled and reduced from four significant statements down to three identifiable themes.

1. Those who experienced "authentic"
leadership felt challenged by their leader.

The first theme was based upon the narrative and conversations involved. This feeling of "being challenged" was grounded in a number of stories wherein the individual was forced, by their leader, to either take on a task they felt ill-equipped for or by allowing them to deal with a difficult task that arose naturally. Though this "pissed off" several of the interviewees and made them feel "overwhelmed" this did not change the perception of the leader's authenticity, rather it intensified it through the emotions experienced.

2. Experiencing "authentic" leadership
provoked emotions of fear which were
followed by a sense of peace.

It was through experiencing "vulnerability," "fatigue," and "fear" that the interviewee began to learn to trust themselves to get the job done. I believe this was an emotional transference felt between the leader and the follower. As the leader not only expressed their trust by allowing the individual to suffer through the situation, they also showed this trust by putting the follower in charge of a task they themselves felt "ill-equipped" to accomplish.

It was through the authority and trust of the leader that the subordinate was able to appropriate this trust and create a sense of self-efficacy. In time, this self-trust came to fruition when the subordinate was not only being given a difficult task, but by conquering the conflict itself. This experience reinforced the trust in both themself and the leader causing the experience to transcend its Situation and enabling the follower to embrace the process of their own growth.

It was shortly after the fatigue and pain that the follower was flooded with emotions described as "relief," "support," "honor," "significance," and "peace." It appears that through the trust of the leader and their own ability to lean on the leader's authority, the follower was challenged, tested, and shaped through the process.

This reinforced the trust for the leader as a repeatable event, which instilled a sense of hope for the future, while simultaneously providing the subordinate with a sense of peace knowing they could potentially meet future challenges set before them. This peace and hope also provided the follower with a sense of honor and significance, which transcended the moment and infected all their future pursuits.

3. Those who experienced "authentic" leadership experienced a sense of transcendence.

The experience of authentic leadership in action provoked a strong sense of transcendence in all those involved making it a strong candidate for universal application. Several interviewees explained their leader "saw something in me I didn't see" as they felt they were "confirmed" in what they were doing, declaring the leader's "fingerprints are now on me…his leadership is still

28

affecting me." This transcendent language speaks to an intuition which is ineffable by bringing the supersensible world into the flesh-and-blood reality one lives in.

The interviewees believed and felt their leader was able to "see" invisible attributes within themselves and this led several to state this same leader was still today having an effect on them. In this case, without knowing it, the interviewees were explaining in some mysterious way that this leader's authenticity was capable of transcending time and space (despite distance, time, and even death in several cases).

This feeling of transcendence came hand-in-hand with a sense of "significance," a feeling that "what I do matters," which came from the followers experience of feeling "free to be real," "hope for the future," and "the joy that comes from being a part of something bigger and participating in it." The transcendence itself was not the key component, it appears that the necessary feelings are "validation," "participation," and a sense of "purpose" that comes from the transcendence of itself.

Conclusion

Authenticity involves three existential aspects: the Self, the Other, and the Situation. The Self lives in its own context, is confronted by the Other, and the stage is the Situation (or the world). Without the Other, authenticity is misunderstood as an individualism of self-fulfillment which is a shallow version of authenticity "sinking to the level of an axiom."[91] Such a proposition falls short of being an universal ideal for one to pursue.[92] Also, without the world there is no context. Based upon this research, a new understanding and model was needed and is provided here.[93]

As a result, I argue that authenticity is not just a quality or a process, but an emergent property that arises from the intersection of a human being's existential journey towards full humanity. This is the application of the wisdom gleaned in the process and guided by one's metaphysical commitments. An experience is deemed authentic if it brings consistency to all aspects of the individual's life which consists of who they are and who they believe themselves to be.[94] Authenticity can be faked and it can be abused, but it is still worth the risk.

---

[91] Taylor, *Ethics of Authenticity*, 17.

[92] Taylor, 14-15.

[93] Taylor, 48.

[94] Archibald D. Hart, *Unlocking the Mystery of Your Emotions*. (New York: W Pub. Group, 1989), 153.

Appendix

A. Choosing a Methodology

The problem with current theories of authenticity is that they lack the "why" of the experience, which may be the reason most scholars are reluctant to define the essence of "authenticity" and those who do try often have to resort to using religious language. This transcendent nature is most likely the reason that authenticity often finds itself compared to a religious experience despite many of these same scholars rejecting religion experience itself. As a counterexample, Susan Skjei applies her training in Buddhism to highlight the deeper meaning of authentic leadership [95] while Paul Tillich prefers to speak of authenticity through the lens of his Christian metaphysic.[96] Regardless, the transcendent and spiritual nature of authenticity is almost undeniable.[97]

Studies have shown the experience of authenticity in the life of a leader's follower is significant and existential as well.[98] Studies show the phenomenon increases the feeling of confidence, hopefulness, and optimism in the subordinate to name a few of its established and documented effects.[99] It is even shown that the leader themself is positively affected by their own perception of being authentic as seen through the eyes of their subordinates who consider them to be authentic,[100] yet this perception of authenticity is never defined in its essential nature; only its effects are recorded. Only a phenomenology is designed for establishing an understanding of the essence of an experience. Through studying

---

[95] Skjei, *Leaders' Lived Experience of Authentic Moments*, 13-214

[96] Tillich, *Systematic Theology*, III 64-66.

[97] Mark Kruger, 773-774.

[98] Andrew Pierce, "Authentic Identities," 442-443.

[99] Weischer, "'To Thine Own Self Be True,'" 482.

[100] Frunză, 31.

the phenomena that shape our perception of the world one can come to grasp the essences of things as well as their deeper meaning.[101]

As a method, phenomenology seeks to grasp the essence of an experience, which is the first step in being able to understand it psychologically. In other words, "phenomenology is identified as a qualitative scientific method that allows the researcher to consider phenomena, which take place in a given person."[102] This method found its origin in the writings of Georg Wilhelm Friedrich Hegel. In his first philosophical text, *Phänomenologie des Geistes*,[103] Hegel attempted to create a description of the stages through which the mind goes from sense perceptions to consciousness of an object to absolute knowledge.[104] Hegel's panrationalism was designed to engage all of reality and to condense it down into one system.[105] As Rollo May explained, "Phenomenology is the endeavour to take the phenomena as given ... the effort to experience instead the phenomena in their full reality as they present themselves."[106]

Phenomenology has no intention of explaining the world; "it wants to be merely a description of actual experience."[107] Phenomenology, though not a source of models and explanations, is by definition the initial building block to an existential understanding of an object or concept. As John Creswell explains, "The basic purpose of phenomenology is to reduce individual experiences with a phenomenon to a description of the universal

---

[101] Cross, 1280.

[102] Guerrero-Castañeda, 2.

[103] Hegel, 38.

[104] Cross, *The Oxford Dictionary of the Christian Church,* 1280.

[105] Rollo May, *Existential Psychology*, 16.

[106] May, *Existential Psychology*, 26.

[107] Albert Camus, 43.

essence."[108] More recently, the philosophical writings of Edmund Husserl and Heidegger have been used to establish phenomenology as a science.

The first step to doing a phenomenology is to bracket one's self. This is the initial work on the part of the researcher to remove his or her own opinions from the experience.[109] This bracketing is followed by data collection. Unlike other types of qualitative study, most phenomenologies are done through interviews only with some possible follow-up via surveys. The data collection often comes from interviews with individuals who have experienced a phenomenon first hand. In such cases, the goal is to locate "significant statements" and to discern from these "meaning units" the "what" and "how" of the experience.

Once the research has been done, the phenomenology ends with a "descriptive passage that discusses the essence of the experience…The essence is the culminating aspect of a phenomenology study."[110] Through this process the researcher will again analyze "the data by reducing the information to significant statements or quotes" and combine the statements into categories or themes. Following this analyzation the researcher will provide a "textural description" of the experiences of the participants with an emphasis on the conditions, situations, and context in order "to convey an overall essence of the experience,"[111] but the phenomenology doesn't end there.

The phenomenologist does not present the reader with a conclusive argument or with a determinate set of ideas, a list of themes, a selection of essences or insights. Instead, the phenomenologist aims to be allusive by orienting the reader

---

[108] Creswell, 76.

[109] Leedy, 141.

[110] Creswell, 79.

[111] Creswell, 80.

reflectively to that region of lived experience where the phenomenon dwells in recognizable form.[112]

---

[112] Van Manen, *Phenomenology of Practice,* 390.

B. Results from the Phenomenology

The research data in this project came from interviews, field notes, surveys, and literary research. The data were broken down into significant statements and four main larger and broad themes were found. Through coding and reduction these themes were broken down further into three specific categories. The selective reduction was the result of reading between the lines and slowly but surely bringing the thoughts of eleven different individuals into union with one another. This reduction resulted in three reduced categories:

(A) the feeling of being challenged
(B) emotions of fear and peace
(C) one's metanarrative and feeling of transcendence.

The phenomenology served me well as themes were found and an essence bubbled to the surface.

BIBLIOGRAPHY

_____. "αὐθέντῃ." *Greek Word Study Tool*. Perseus Digital Library. www.perseus.tufts.edu. www.perseus.tufts.edu/hopper/morph?l=au%29qe%2Fnths&la= greek&can=au%29qe%2Fnths0#lexicon (accessed June 15, 2018).

_____. "Authentic." Online Etymology Dictionary. www.etymonline.com. www.etymonline.com/word/authentic (accessed July 10, 2018).

Aristotle and Hugh Lawson-Tancred. *Metaphysics*. London: Penguin Books, 2004.

Aristotle. "Metaphysics: book 1, section 983b." www.perseus.tufts.edu. www.perseus.tufts.edu/hopper/text?doc=Perseus:text:1999.01.00 52:book=1:section=983b (May 4, 2017).

Aristotle, James Alexander, Kerr Thomson, Hugh Tredennick, and Jonathan Barnes. *The Nicomachean Ethics*. London: Penguin Books, 2004.

Bandura, Albert. "Self-Efficacy Defined," www.uky.edu. www.uky.edu/~eushe2/Bandura/BanEncy.html (accessed July 1, 2018).

Camus, Albert, and Justin O'Brien. *The Myth of Sisyphus, and Other Essays*. New York: Vintage Books, 1991.

Cardon, Melissa S. "Is Passion Contagious? The Transference of Entrepreneurial Passion to Employees." *Human Resource Management Review* 18, no. 2 (2008): 77–86.

Cicero. *The Letters of Cicero: the Whole Extant Correspondence in Chronological Order in Four Volumes*. Edited by E. Shuckburgh. Medford, MA: George Bell and Sons, 1909.

Clark, David W. "A Preliminary Investigation and Critique of the Ethics of Dietrich Bonhoeffer," Master's Thesis, Loyola University

Chicago, 1968. https://ecommons.luc.edu/luc_theses/2118/.

Cohen, Marc S., Patricia Curd, and C.D. Reeve (Eds). *Reading in Ancient Greek Philosophy.* 2nd ed. Indianapolis, IN: Hackett Publishing Company, Inc., 2000.

Creswell, John. *Qualitative Inquiry and Research Design Choosing among Five Approaches 3rd ed.* London: Sage, 2012.

Cross, F.L., and E.A. Livingstone (Eds.). *The Oxford dictionary of the Christian Church* 3rd ed. New York: Oxford University Press, 2005.

Dewey, John. *Experience and Education.* New York: Simon & Schuster, 1997.

Euripides, *"*The Trojan Women by Euripides," *The Internet Classics Archive,* www. Classics.mit.edu. http://classics.mit.edu/Euripides/troj_women.html, (accessed June 24, 2018).

Farahmandfar, Masoud, and Gholamreza Samigorganroodi, "'To Thine Own Self Be True': Existentialism in Hamlet and The Blind Owl," *International Journal of Comparative Literature & Translation Studies* Vol. 3 No. 2; April 2015: 25-31.

Freeman, R. Edward, and Ellen R. Auster. "Values, Authenticity, and Responsible Leadership." *Responsible Leadership* (2011): 15–23.

Friedeman, C. T. "Authoritative Teaching." In *The Lexham Bible Dictionary.* Bellingham, WA: Lexham Press, 2016.

Friedman, Edwin H., Margaret M. Treadwell, and Edward W. Beal. *A Failure of Nerve: Leadership in the Age of the Quick Fix.* New York: Church Publishing, 2017.

Frunză, Sandu. "Seeking Meaning, Living Authenticity and Leadership in Public Space. A Philosophical Perspective." *Transylvanian Review of Administrative Sciences* no. 52E (2017): 23–37.

Gardner, William L., Dawn Fischer, and James G. Hunt, "Emotional

Labor and Leadership: A Threat to Authenticity?," *The Leadership Quarterly* 20 (2009): 466–482.

Gazzianiga, Michael S. and Steven Megan S. *Neuroscience and the Law: Brain, Mind, and the Scales of Justice*. New York, NY: Dana Press, 2005.

Greenleaf, Robert K., and Larry C. Spears. *Servant Leadership: a Journey into the Nature of Legitimate Power and Greatness*. Paulist Press, 2002. Kindle.

Grene, Marjorie. "Authenticity: An Existential Virtue." *Ethics* 62, no. 4 (1952): 266–274.

Guerrero-Castañeda, Raúl Fernando, Tânia Maria de Oliva Menezes, and Guadalupe Ojeda-Varga, "Characteristics of the Phenomenological Interview in Nursing Research," *Revista Gaúcha de Enfermagem*, 38 (2), (2017).

Hargrave, Terry D., and Franz Pfitzer. *Restoration Therapy: Understanding and Guiding Healing in Marriage and Family Therapy*. New York: Brunner-Routledge, 2011.

Hart, Archibald D. *Unlocking the Mystery of Your Emotions*. Dallas: Word, 1989.

Hazlitt, William. www. Absoluteshakespeare.com, www.absoluteshakespeare.com/guides/essays/othello_characters_essay.htm (accessed Oct 1, 2018).

Hegel, George Wilhelm Friedrich, and M. J. Inwood. *Hegel: the Phenomenology of Spirit*. Oxford: Oxford University Press, 2018.

Kruger, Mark, and Yvonne Seng, "Leadership with Inner Meaning: A Contingency Theory of Leadership based on the Worldviews of Five Religions" *The Leadership Quarterly* 16 (2005): 771–806.

Leedy, Paul and Jeanne Ellis Ormrod. *Practical Research: Planning and Design, 9th Ed*. Bellevue, WA: Content Technologies, 2009.

Lewis, C. S. *Miracles: A Preliminary Study*. New York:

HarperSanFrancisco, 2001.

Liddell, H.G. and R. Scott. *Greek-English Lexicon*. 9th ed. New York, NY: Oxford University Press, 1996.

MacRae, George W. (translator), *Authoritative Teaching -- The Nag Hammadi Library*. www.gnosis.org. http://gnosis.org/naghamm/autho.html (accessed July 1 2018).

Maritain, Jacques, and Galantière Lewis. *Existence and the Existent*. Garden City, NY: Image Books, 1956.

May, Rollo. *Existential Psychology*. New York: Random House, 1969.

Pierce, Andrew J. "Authentic Identities." *Social Theory and Practice* 41, no. 3 (2015): 442-443.

Pinker, Steven. *The Stuff of Thought: Language as a Window into Human Nature*. New York: Viking, 2007.

Raffo, Deana M. "Reflection and Authentic Leadership (Chapter Eight)." In *Leading with Spirit, Presence, and Authenticity: A Volume in the International Leadership Association Series Building Leadership Bridges*, Edited by Kathryn Goldman Schuyler. John Wiley & Sons, Incorporated, 2014. ProQuest Ebook Central.

Roberts, David E. *Psychotherapy and a Christian View of Man*. New York: Greenwood Press, 1990.

Russell, Bertrand. *Why I am Not a Christian: and other essays on religion and related subjects*. New York: George Allen & Unwin LTD, 1957.

Séneca and Moses Hadas. *The Stoic Philosophy of Seneca: Essays and Letters of Seneca*. New York: The Norton Library, 1968.

Shakespeare, William. *Hamlet*. Kindle Edition: OPU, 2018.

Skjei, Susan. "Leaders' Lived Experience of Authentic Moments (Chapter Ten)," In *Leading with Spirit, Presence, and Authenticity: A Volume in the International Leadership Association Series Building Leadership Bridges*, Edited by

Kathryn Goldman Schuyler. John Wiley & Sons, Incorporated, 2014. ProQuest Ebook Central, 213-231.

Smedes, Lewis B. *Shame and Grace: Healing the Shame We Don't Deserve*. New York: Harper San Francisco, 1993.

Taylor, Charles. *The Ethics of Authenticity*. Cambridge: Belknap Press, 1991.

Taylor, Charles. *A Secular Age*. Cambridge: Belknap Press, 2007.

Tillich, Paul. *The Courage to Be*. New Haven, CT: Yale University Press, 1952.

Tillich, Paul. *Love, Power, Justice*. Cambridge: Oxford Press, 1960.

Tolstoy, Leo, and Jane Kentish. *A Confession and Other Religious Writings*. Middlesex, England: Penguin, 1987.

Vanhoozer, Kevin J. *Is There a Meaning in This Text?: the Bible, the Reader, and the Morality of Literary Knowledge*. Grand Rapids, MI: Zondervan, 1998.

Van Manen, Max. "Phenomenology in Its Original Sense," *Qualitative Health Research* , Vol. 27(6), (2017): 810 –825.

Weischer, Anna Elisabeth, Jürgen Weibler, and Malte Petersen. "'To Thine Own Self Be True': The Effects of Enactment and Life Storytelling on Perceived Leader Authenticity." *The Leadership Quarterly* 24, no. 4 (2013): 477–495.

Westfall, Cynthia Long. "The Meaning of αὐθεντέω in I Timothy 2:12," *Journal of Greco-Roman Christianity and Judaism*, 10 (2014): 138-73.

Young, Benjamin. "A Qualitative Study of Doubt in the Evangelical Tradition." DMin Thesis. Bethel Seminary, St. Paul, 2015. Accessed March 21, 2018, CLIC Thesis (9910123312903692).

Printed in Great Britain
by Amazon